What Happens to GARBAGE?

Books by Rona Beame

WHAT HAPPENS TO GARBAGE?

LADDER COMPANY 108

CALLING CAR 24 FRANK
   A Day with The Police

What Happens to GARBAGE?

Written and Photographed **by Rona Beame**

Julian Messner **New York**

Published by Julian Messner, a Division of Simon & Schuster, Inc.
1 West 39 Street, New York, N.Y. 10018. All rights reserved.
Copyright © 1975 by Rona Beame
Printed in the United States of America
Design by Alex D'Amato
Photographs on pages 59-60 courtesy of
Combustion Engineering, Inc.

Library of Congress Cataloging in Publication Data
Beame, Rona.
    What happens to garbage?
    SUMMARY: Discusses the means used by New York
City to dispose of its refuse.
    1. Refuse and refuse disposal—New York (City)—
Juvenile literature. 2. Recycling (Waste, etc.)—
Juvenile literature. [1. Refuse and refuse dis-
posal—New York (City) 2. Recycling (Waste)]
I. Title
HD4484.N7B4   363.6   75-22331
ISBN 0-671-32760-7
ISBN 0-671-32761-5 lib. bdg.

For my mother-
and father-in-law
with love

contents

chapter 1

Picking Up the Garbage

*I*t is 6 o'clock in the morning, and most of New York City is still asleep. But in garages all over the city, the sanitation men are getting their trucks ready. Soon 1400 sanitation trucks will be out on the city streets.

One of the trucks is driven by Orazio Dimaiuta, nicknamed "Dee." He has been in the Sanitation Department for 15 years and is very proud of his work.

There are two loaders on the truck. Arthur Papa, "Pappy," has been with the Sanitation Department for 26 years. He is full of good stories and laughs. Vincent Campanella, "Vinnie," is the youngest. He has curly black hair, a black moustache, and an easy smile.

The route of their truck is on the upper west

side of Manhattan. Most of the buildings there have superintendents who take care of them. It is the "super's" job to put out the garbage in cans or large plastic bags.

Pappy and Vinnie hop out of the cab of the

truck and go to work. They carry the heavy cans and bulging plastic bags over to the truck. They drop the bags into the open "mouth" in back, and then lift the heavy cans high to pour out the garbage.

When the "mouth" is full, Vinnie pulls a lever. A huge iron blade pushes the garbage towards the front of the truck, crushing it together, so that it takes up less room. Now more garbage can be dumped in back. The truck makes a grinding noise which sounds very loud in the early morning.

Vinnie and Pappy go from building to building, collecting the garbage, while Dee slowly follows in the truck. When they get to the larger buildings, where there may be 15 or more full cans of garbage, Dee jumps out to help.

They reach Riverside Drive, which runs along the Hudson River.

"They call this the Eskimo run," Pappy says. "In the winter, the wind comes off the river so hard it can knock a man down."

"The cold sure gets to your fingers and toes," Vinnie adds. "And the rain isn't too much fun either. But a sunny day like today is something else. I like being outdoors with the sun on my face. I could never work at a desk."

They turn off Riverside Drive into a narrow side street. Cars are tightly parked on both sides, and there isn't enough space to bring the cans through. So Vinnie lifts them up over the cars and gives them to Pappy who is standing by the truck.

"The cars are only supposed to park on one side of the street so that we can pick up the garbage, and the guys with the mechanical brooms can clean the empty side," Pappy says. "But there are always some jokers who don't pay attention to the laws.

"The sanitation police keep giving them tickets, but I guess they don't care. Look, there's one of our guys now." Pappy points up the street to a sanitation policeman on a scooter.

"Hey, Pappy, look at this," Vinnie shouts from across the street. He is prancing around with a broken umbrella.

"You look very sweet, my dear," Pappy jokes.

Vinnie throws the umbrella into the back of the truck with everything else. Then a minute later, he says:

"Look what's in this can!" He is holding a can filled with used hypodermic needles.

"Some doctor couldn't be bothered to pack them in something," Vinnie says angrily. "Those needles are dangerous. They carry all kinds of germs. And if you get stuck, you can get pretty sick. Last year, 800 of our guys were stuck by needles.

"You have to watch out for broken glass, too. When you're working quickly, you don't see it sticking out of the plastic bags and you get cut. A few months ago, I had to get ten stitches in my arm."

"There are a lot of goodies in the garbage," Pappy says, as he carries some boxes over to the truck, helped by one of the neighborhood children. "Once I picked up some garbage and felt something soft under my arm. Then it moved. I started to sweat because I knew I had a handlock on a rat. Feh! You also see a lot of roaches."

The truck is filling fast and soon has its full load —five tons of garbage. Dee drives the truck to the 59th Street terminal to dump the load. The truck goes to the terminal two times a day. While it is gone, Vinnie and Pappy sweep the streets with their brooms.

"People lose all kinds of things in their garbage," Pappy says. "Diamond rings, money, important papers—even false teeth. One man's teeth fell off the sink into the garbage. Before he discovered

what had happened, the garbage was put out and collected.

"He was very upset and called the Sanitation Department to ask if they could find his teeth. The truck was brought to the terminal and all the garbage in it was dumped out onto the concrete floor. And believe it or not, they found his teeth!"

Dee drives the empty truck back to meet Vinnie and Pappy. They have brought their lunches, and go to a nearby sanitation center to eat.

The center is in a very old, run-down building on Amsterdam Avenue. It is one long narrow room with lockers, a shower, and two toilets. The room is dirty-looking. The paint is peeling, the plaster cracked. They sit on hard wooden benches to eat their lunch.

"It's awful," Dee says. "We know it, but it's all we can get. No one wants the garbage trucks parked in their neighborhood. So we have to eat our lunch, change our clothes and shower at the end of the day in this roachy place.

"But you know what," Dee adds, "even with this ugly place and all the jokes about us, most of us like the job. It's a hard job. But it's a good job, and it pays well. It's good to work out in the fresh air, and each day you know you've accomplished something —what would the city do without us?"

chapter 2

The Largest Dump in the World

Meanwhile, what has happened to the garbage Dee has dumped? What does New York City do with the thousands of tons of garbage it collects each day?

As Dee pulls up to the 59th Street Terminal on the Hudson River, his truck is weighed on a scale before the garbage is dumped. In this way, the Sanitation Department knows exactly how much garbage is being handled and where it goes.

The terminal is one of nine such stations. It is a huge, dark place. Dee backs the truck to the edge of the pier and opens up the back of the truck. A large blade is set in motion and pushes the garbage out of the truck into a barge waiting 20 feet below in the water.

Tons of garbage rush out of Dee's truck. The dust from the garbage rises in huge clouds. Jets of water are sprayed on the garbage to hold down the dust and to guard against fires.

A barge usually carries about 650 tons of garbage. When it is filled, it is towed to Fresh Kills, a swampy area on Staten Island. One-third of all the city's garbage goes by barge to Fresh Kills. It is 3,000 acres and is the largest landfill in the world.

A landfill is an area where garbage is dumped, flattened by bulldozers, and then covered with at least six inches of earth every day. This cuts down the smell and keeps the rats away. New York City has eight landfills, all run by the Sanitation Department.

The nine terminals, or barge stations, supply Fresh Kills with 10,000 tons of garbage each day. Most of it is raw garbage—the garbage that we throw out. But some of it has been burned first. Seventeen percent of the city's garbage goes to incinerators for burning before going to the landfills.

At the incinerators, the garbage is burned in huge furnaces which turn 100 pounds of raw garbage into 20 pounds of ashes. This saves a lot of landfill space. But incineration is expensive and there are only six incinerators in the city—only enough to burn 5,000 tons of garbage a day.

The ashes are loaded onto the barges at the incinerators.

As a barge approaches Fresh Kills, the fore-man, who works in a control tower, directs it in. When the barge reaches the dock, a crane scoops the garbage out and puts it into Athey Wagons—open garbage bins on treads.

The Athey Wagons are drawn by tractors from the dock to the "active bank," the area of the landfill that is now ready for dumping. (Each landfill is designed by an engineer who decides where each slope and flat level will be.)

The Athey Wagons creep across the land-scape of garbage with rags, papers, and plastic bags hanging over the sides—some of it dropping off along the way.

As you look around Fresh Kills, there is garbage as far as your eyes can see. There are no trees and no grass, and the land is flat, except for some hills of garbage.

You see plastic bags everywhere—green ones, clear ones, white ones. You look closer at the garbage, and see broken dolls, bits of clothing, and old letters that only the rats will read now.

The food, paper, and rags will eventually rot and become part of the soil. But the plastic bags and aluminum cans will take centuries to rot or decompose.

Then you notice the rubber tires. They are everywhere. The sanitation men who work at Fresh Kills say that no matter how deeply the tires are buried, they always work their way to the surface, inch by inch. The men think that the vibrations of the heavy machinery does it.

But most of all you notice the smell—the smell of rotting garbage. And the heat of summer makes

the smell even stronger. Yet the men who work here say the smell doesn't bother them—that after a while they don't even notice it.

When the Athey Wagons dump their loads on the active bank, the land at Fresh Kills becomes a little higher. Most of New York City is near sea level. But Fresh Kills is now 30 to 40 feet above sea level. The city government has set 50 to 70 feet as the limit for Fresh Kills.

"When it reaches that point, the city will close Fresh Kills as a landfill. The land will be used for parks and industrial development," explains Dick Napoli, a public information officer in the Sanitation Department.

"If we let Fresh Kills get too high, the land won't be usable. You need flat areas for a park. You can't put baseball fields and parking lots on the slopes of a mountain."

But what is Fresh Kills doing to the land and water around it?

When rainwater seeps through rotting garbage in a landfill, it picks up germs and chemicals. That water, now polluted, eventually finds its way into the surrounding waters, polluting them. And in some areas of the country polluted rain water from landfills ends up in the drinking water.

Even in a well-designed landfill with drainage pipes and ditches, there is no way to stop some of the rainwater from soaking through the landfill.

"But there is no way we will ever know how much Fresh Kills has polluted Staten Island's waters because those waters are also being polluted by industry and untreated sewage from homes," Napoli says.

Chuck Macaluso, a man who has spent his whole life working with garbage, says:

"I feel very happy for the people in Ohio because they're 500 miles away from Fresh Kills. Five years ago, the health department banned swimming here. Now they've banned fishing and clamming. Staten Island's coastline has been ruined by Fresh Kills.

"You can't ever have a landfill that doesn't pollute. Unfortunately, up to now, our cities have had no choice. There was no other place to put the garbage. There was just the landfills."

chapter 3

Garbage and Sea Gulls

At Fountain Avenue, in Brooklyn, there is another landfill. It is one of the city's seven landfills where garbage is brought in by trucks. Fountain Avenue is much smaller than Fresh Kills—it is 300 acres. Still, it is the largest truckfill in the world.

From a distance, the Fountain Avenue landfill looks beautiful. It sits high on cliffs overlooking Jamaica Bay, an inlet of the Atlantic Ocean. The sky on this summer day is bright blue and the water sparkles in the sun. Then you notice the Sanitation Department trucks scurrying around like ants on top of the cliffs.

As you get closer, you see the trucks dumping their loads of garbage. They bring in 5,000 tons of garbage each day. Special trucks spray the garbage with deodorant and disinfectant. But even so, the garbage still smells.

Bulldozers spread and flatten the big mounds of garbage. Then the earth-movers bury the garbage. They push six inches of soil over every ten feet of garbage.

As you watch all the big machines moving slowly over the garbage, Fountain Avenue seems more like a colony on the planet Mars than a part of New York City.

But the most spectacular thing about Fountain Avenue are the sea gulls. There are thousands and thousands of them swirling and swooping over the garbage. In the sky, they are beautiful to watch, but on the ground, clawing at the garbage, they are ugly.

"The sea gulls are rats with wings," says James Bove, the foreman of Fountain Avenue. "They'll eat anything, even glass. They look like they're all over the place, but actually they only fly around the active bank, right where we're dumping."

There are many different things going on at Fountain Avenue. Below one hill of garbage is an animal graveyard. That seems rather strange until you think about it.

What can be done with the zoo elephant who dies? Or the hippopotamus? Or a policeman's horse that breaks its leg and has to be shot? Or the 500 pigs in the city's meat market that have gotten a disease and have to be killed?

A special sanitation truck collects them and carts them out to the landfills where they are buried.

Another area, flat and open, is littered with broken chairs, three-legged tables, and ripped mattresses. It is the place where people can bring their old or worn-out furniture for dumping.

Still another area is filled with discarded metal —old refrigerators, stoves, and cabinets. But the metal will not be wasted. New York City has a contract with a company that buys and sells scrap metal. Using a huge magnetic crane, the scrap dealer lifts out those metals he can sell. He pays the city for the metal, and saves the city a great deal of landfill space.

And so the earth at Fountain Avenue receives all the things we no longer want or need. The animals, the food, wood and metal that once came from the earth will now return to it.

One day, when the city closes the landfill, those millions of tons of cans, bottles, food, and paper will be covered with two feet of soil and planted with grass. Fountain Avenue will become a park, a part of Gateway National Park, with baseball fields, picnic areas and playgrounds.

New York City already has parks, golf courses,

and even airports built on old landfills. Do you think
people who use them realize that they are walking on
top of garbage?

chapter 4

Where Old Buildings Get Buried

Like old furniture, buildings wear out too. They become rundown or just too old, and have to make way for newer, bigger buildings. Then,

wrecking crews come and pound them to pieces.

Well, what happens to the pieces? What happens to the old bricks, concrete blocks, steel beams, and glass? It is all loaded on trucks and brought to a special landfill, used only for construction waste.

There are four such landfills in New York City, and one of them is at Pennsylvania Avenue. It is right next to the Fountain Avenue landfill, but it seems so different. The Pennsylvania Avenue landfill doesn't smell.

John Cassiliano runs Pennsylvania Avenue. Everyone calls him Johnny Cass. His office is in a trailer. Around it is a marvelous assortment of plants —tomatoes, squash, peppers, melons, and all kinds of flowers.

"We started with 110 acres of nothing here," Johnny Cass explains. "We figured we had to accommodate between six and eight million yards (4 billion pounds) of construction waste. With that much waste, the only way we could go was up. And that's just what we did." He points to the large hills in front of his trailer. "We're now at 60 feet."

"But we're not just dumping the stuff at random. Everything is planned. We know just where we're going to build hills and where the flat areas will be. We even know which flat area is going to be a baseball field and which will be a parking lot.

"Before this, it took years to turn a landfill into something else. But when this landfill closes, it will be all ready to be made into a park. We'll be part of Gateway National Park, just like Fountain Avenue.

"As we finish each area, we plant it. That's
never been done before, either. And everyone in the
community is helping us plant. Right now the Girl
Scouts are planting marsh grass down by the water.
The marsh grass will help keep the shoreline from
washing away."

As Johnny is talking, a man leads a horse and two goats across the landfill.

"How do you like my pets?" he asks, laughing. "When the director of operations came here he happened to see some of my animals.

" 'What's that?' he asked me.

" 'Just my pets—a small horse, two goats, a couple of ducks and some dogs,' I told him. 'We found them here and gave them food and water. We couldn't let them starve, could we?'

"He didn't believe me, but what could he say? So he just shrugged. I didn't tell him about our bee hive. If I did he would have been sure we were crazy."

Johnny points to a large hill with an earth road winding around it. He calls it his "mountain." From the top of his mountain, he looks out over Pennsylvania Avenue. Johnny watches a bulldozer below make a cloud of dust as it levels out the construction waste.

"We're actually making a new landscape here with construction waste," he says. "This place is one of the greatest satisfactions of my life. I'm old enough to retire now, but I started this job and I'm going to finish it.

"And when it's finished, I'll put a flag on top of my mountain and throw the biggest party you ever saw."

chapter 5

Other Kinds of Garbage

Everything we do creates garbage: the food we leave over, the test papers we write in school, the letters we receive, and the infected tonsils that are removed in a hospital. All of it must be disposed of.

The Sanitation Department collects garbage from homes and from city institutions like schools, museums, public hospitals, and libraries.

But office buildings, factories, stores, restaurants, and construction companies must pay to have their garbage removed by private sanitation companies. These companies take the garbage to the city landfills where they pay to dump it.

One of the private sanitation companies is New York Carting Company, which collects 1,000 tons of garbage a day from restaurants, office buildings, and

even from the Statue of Liberty. Chuck Macaluso is one of the owners of the company.

"Some of the buildings we service have 18,000 people working there—in just one building," he says. "That's hard to imagine because there are a lot of towns in this country that have less than 18,000 people living in them.

"That many people make a lot of garbage— 48,000 pounds a day. Ten thousand pounds is food and the rest is paper. And all of it has to be removed each day.

"New York City throws away mountains of paper each day. Take banks, Wall Street, advertising companies. They all use up huge amounts of paper. Everything they do uses up paper.

"We pick up the paper at night and bring it to a paper recycling plant—Collabella Brothers in New Jersey."

The main floor at Collabella Brothers looks like a sea of paper. In the middle of that sea, two men rake the paper onto a conveyer belt. The paper is then shredded, baled, and sold to paper mills which will recycle it into new paper.

Cars become garbage, too. Last year 51,000 cars were abandoned on New York City's streets. The city sells them to companies who tow them away to places that recycle metal.

"Metal recycling is a lot more exciting to watch than paper recycling," Macaluso says. "There's a really extraordinary place in Brooklyn that recycles metals. It's called Schiabo-Neu."

High gates surround Schiabo-Neu. Every day enormous trucks loaded with 1,000 old cars pass through those gates. Once inside, everywhere you look, there are cars. Some of the cars lie on their backs, some are stacked on top of each other, and some are squashed like flattened tin cans.

Three cranes swoop down on the cars, grabbing and lifting them across this auto graveyard, and then dropping them onto a conveyer belt. A moment later, the cars are gone, swallowed up in a large building. There, 20 enormous hammers pound the cars and shred them into small pieces.

"It only takes 18 seconds for us to chop up a car," explains a foreman at Schiabo-Neu. "The upholstery and dirt are separated from the steel, so when the metal leaves our plant it is a clean product. It just has to be melted down.

"We ship the steel to Europe and Japan where it is made into new cars. Then the whole thing starts all over again."

At the back of the large building, small chunks of metal drop out of a chute into a barge in the water below.

"There go your Fords and Cadillacs," Macaluso says, laughing.

Recycling cars is one way to conserve metal. In fact, all of our natural resources can be conserved by recycling. Governments on every level can help. They can pass laws requiring that newspapers, cans, and bottles be recycled. And they can encourage manufacturers to recycle, by lowering taxes on recycled goods.

We have to stop making so much garbage! As consumers, the people who do the buying, we can help. We can stop buying paper plates and towels and all the other things we use once and then throw away. We can sort our garbage and take recyclables —material that can be recycled—to special collection centers. And we can insist on products that are made with recyclable materials. We, as consumers, have a lot of power to help conserve our country's resources.

chapter 6

What Will We Do With Our Garbage?

What will we do with our garbage? That is the question everybody who works with garbage is thinking about, talking about, and worrying about. Because they all know that not only are we running out of places to put our garbage, we are also running out of time.

New York City has eight landfills and all of them are scheduled to close by 1985. What will the city do with its garbage then? Thirty thousand tons of garbage is a lot of garbage to get rid of each day.

New landfills are out of the question. There just isn't enough vacant land close to the city that can be used for landfills.

Big cities like New York have to come up with new and better ways of getting rid of their garbage.

They're all working on ways to take out the recyclables and to use the rest of the garbage as fuel. Garbage is not bad as fuel—a ton of garbage will make as much heat as one-third ton of coal.

Several plants in the United States are already using garbage as fuel. In a refuse plant in St. Louis, Missouri, the garbage is placed on a conveyor belt which takes it to a giant hammermill. The hammermill pounds the garbage into tiny pieces. The metals are then removed for recycling, and the rest of the garbage is burned as fuel.

But, so far, none of the plants have been able to process more than 150 tons of garbage for fuel per day. This is not much when you think New York City must get rid of 30,000 tons a day.

New York is one of the cities planning to burn garbage as fuel. It will build a plant on Staten Island where garbage will be shredded and the recyclables taken out. Then the shredded garbage will go to the boilers of the nearby Con Edison plant (an electric and gas company). There it will be burned along with oil or coal to create steam which spins the turbines which make electricity. The city expects to dispose of 1,200 tons of garbage a day this way.

"The Staten Island project looks very good," says Arthur Price, Director of Waste Disposal in the Sanitation Department. "But it won't be ready for a couple of years, and it'll be many years before we can possibly dispose of all the garbage New York City produces.

"So we've got to find someplace to put our garbage while we work on the long-term solutions. Our first job is to keep the landfills going as long as possible. To save landfill space, we're recycling everything we can. For instance, at the Marine Transfer station in the Bronx, we set aside the bulk metal picked up by our trucks and barge it to Schiabo-Neu.

"We've also started collecting newspapers for

recycling. We've put racks underneath our garbage trucks so that we can pick up the papers when we collect the garbage.

"We also have a plan to use garbage to fill in abandoned mines. We would pay a private company to bale our garbage and ship it to states like Ohio and West Virginia where there are many old mines. I hope it works out. But in a few cases where this was tried, someone did complain, 'You can't ship your garbage through my town.'"

"For a long time, the city just fumbled along, hoping their landfills would last forever," says Martin Lang, a very energetic man who is now hard at work setting up a long-range plan for what New York City will do with its garbage.

"These projects take a long time from planning to completion—about eight years. So we've got to get started right now. And we are.

"We'll build the shredding plant on Staten Island, and at the same time we'll be planning bigger and better plants. Sure, we'll make mistakes. But don't forget—we're like explorers in a new world. We're charting a whole new future for garbage, and," Lang smiles, "it better work."